Comparing Minibeasts

# Minibeasts on the Move

## Charlotte Guillain

Raintree

**www.raintreepublishers.co.uk**
Visit our website to find out
more information about
Raintree books.

**To order:**

☎ Phone 0845 6044371

🖹 Fax +44 (0) 1865 312263

🖳 Email myorders@raintreepublishers.co.uk

Customers from outside the UK please telephone +44 1865 312262

Raintree is an imprint of Capstone Global Library Limited, a company incorporated in England and Wales having its registered office at 7 Pilgrim Street, London, EC4V 6LB – Registered company number: 6695582

Edited by Nancy Dickmann and Catherine Veitch
Designed by Joanna Hinton-Malivoire
Picture research by Elizabeth Alexander
Production by Duncan Gilbert and Victoria Fitzgerald
Originated by Heinemann Library
Printed and bound in China by South China Printing Company Ltd

ISBN 978 0 431 19495 0 (hardback)
14 13 12 11 10
10 9 8 7 6 5 4 3 2 1

ISBN 978 0 431 19502 5 (paperback)
15 14 13 12 11
10 9 8 7 6 5 4 3 2

**British Library Cataloguing in Publication Data**
Guillain, Charlotte.
Comparing minibeasts.
On the move.
592.1'479-dc22

**Acknowledgements**
We would would like to thank the following for permission to reproduce photographs: Alamy pp. **15** (© Arco Images GmbH), **18** (© mike lane), **21** (© blickwinkel); Corbis pp. **7** (© Ludovic Maisant), **14** (© Papilio); FLPA pp. **8** (Thomas Marent/Minden Pictures), **10** (Michael Durham/Minden Pictures), **20** (Foto Natura Stock), **23 middle** (Foto Natura Stock); iStockphoto pp. **6** (© Alasdair Thomson), **16** (© Robert Harnden), **22 left** (© Tomasz Zachariasz), **23 top** (© Alasdair Thomson); Photolibrary pp. **4** (moodboard), **5** (Motor-Presse Syndication /Superstock), **11** (Paulo de Oliveira/OSF), **12** (Anton Luhr/imagebroker.net), **13** (Satoshi Kuribayashi/OSF), **17** (André Skonieczny/imagebroker.net), **19** (Colin Milkins/OSF); Shutterstock pp. **9** (© orionmystery@flickr), **22 top right** (© Potapov Alexander), **22 bottom right** (© Dole), **23 bottom** (© Yellowj).

Cover photograph of leaping grasshoppers reproduced with permission of NHPA (Stephen Dalton). Back cover photograph of an ant reproduced with permission of Shutterstock (© orionmystery@flickr).

The publishers would like to thank Nancy Harris and Kate Wilson for their assistance in the preparation of this book.

Every effort has been made to contact copyright holders of material reproduced in this book. Any omissions will be rectified in subsequent printings if notice is given to the publishers.

# Contents

# Meet the minibeasts

There are many different types of minibeasts.

Minibeasts move in many
different ways.

# Crawling and running

Some minibeasts crawl.

Some minibeasts run quickly.

legs

Millipedes run on many legs.

legs

Ants run on six legs.

# Jumping

Grasshoppers can jump.

Fleas can jump a very long way.

back legs

Crickets can jump with two strong back legs.

Jumping spiders have eight strong legs to help them jump.

# Flying

Many insects can fly.

wing

They use wings to fly.

Hawkmoths fly quickly.

Bumblebees fly slowly.

# Swimming

Many insects can swim in water.

back legs

Diving beetles use their back legs
to swim.

Water boatmen swim under
the water.

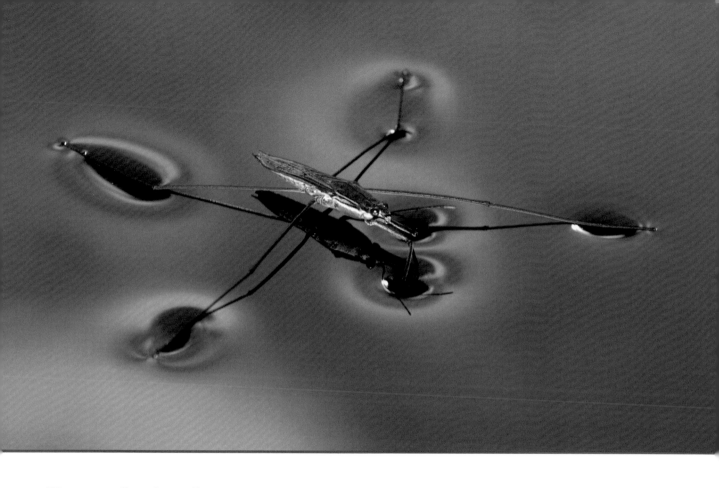

Pond skaters move on top of
the water.

# How big?

ant

cricket

butterfly

Look at how big some of the minibeasts in this book can be.

# Picture glossary

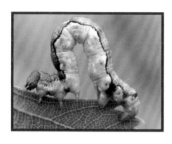 **crawl** move forward by dragging the body close to the ground

 **dive** go into water headfirst

 **insect** very small creature with six legs

# Index

**Notes to parents and teachers**

**Before reading**

Make a list of minibeasts with the children. Try to include insects, arachnids (e.g. spiders), crustaceans (e.g. woodlice), myriapods (e.g. centipedes and millipedes), earthworms, slugs, and snails. Do they know how each minibeast moves? Can they name any minibeasts that fly? Can they think of any minibeasts that crawl or swim?

**After reading**

• Listen to *Flight of the Bumblebee* by Rimsky-Korsakov. Before you play it do not tell the children the name of the piece and ask them to guess which insect the music is about. Afterwards tell them the name and ask if they think it sounded like a bumblebee. You could also listen to *The Wasps* by Vaughan Williams.

• Work out a minibeast dance together. Ask the children to scuttle quickly and crawl slowly, to jump, and pretend to fly and swim. You could make minibeast masks and costumes to perform the dance.

• Take the children to hunt minibeasts on the move. Help them to peel back bark on rotten logs, look under stones, look for worms in soil, or find caterpillars on leaves, as well as looking for flying insects. What types of minibeasts can they find? How do they move? Help the children draw comparisons between different minibeasts.